23.70

PEOPLE AT
THE CENTER OF

THE RUSSIAN REVOLUTION

By BRITTA BJORNLUND

BLACKBIRCH PRESS

An imprint of Thomson Gale, a part of The Thomson Corporation

THOMSON

GALE

Detroit • New York • San Francisco • San Diego • New Haven, Conn. • Waterville, Maine • London • Munich

LIBRARY OF CONGRESS CATALOGING-IN-PUBLICATION DATA

Bjornlund, Britta.
  The Russian Revolution / by Britta Bjornlund.
    p. cm. — (People at the center of)
  ISBN 1-56711-923-9 (hardcover : alk. paper)
  1. Revolutionaries—Russia—Biography—Juvenile literature. 2. Russia—Biography—Juvenile literature. 3. Soviet Union—History—Revolution, 1917–1921—Juvenile literature. 4. Russia—History—Nicholas II, 1894–1917—Juvenile literature. I. Title. II. Series.
  DK253.B558 2005
  947.084'1'0922—dc22
                                                                2004017612

CONTENTS

PEOPLE AT THE CENTER OF

THE RUSSIAN REVOLUTION

The Russian Revolution of 1917 was a monumental event in Russian history. A series of uprisings caused the collapse of a three-hundred-year-old family-run empire and ultimately established a radically new one-party system. The revolution consisted of two stages—the February Revolution, which resulted in the resignation of Tsar Nicholas II, and the October Revolution, during which a group called the Bolsheviks took control of the government.

At the turn of the twentieth century, over 125 million people lived in the Russian empire. They were ruled by a tsar, who was an all-powerful monarch. There were no legal political parties and no elected legislature. The tsar had limitless power, and those who opposed him were often arrested, sent into exile to live in Siberia, or killed.

Russia's class structure included a wealthy, landowning upper class and a very poor peasant class that worked the land. In the 1890s, Russia underwent a rapid industrialization process; many peasants left farms to work in new factories. Continued poverty and poor working conditions in the factories led to unrest, and workers' strikes were common.

In the 1880s, a group known as Marxists emerged in Russia's upper class. Marxists, drawing on the theories of German philosopher Karl Marx, argued that socialism, the economic system based on public ownership of all goods and services, would come about in Russia through revolution. Many Marxists organized themselves illegally as the Russian Social Democratic Labor Party (SDLP). In 1903, tensions erupted between two party members, Vladimir Ilyich Lenin and Georgii Plekhanov. This caused a split in the party between the Bolsheviks and Mensheviks. The Bolsheviks were led by Lenin, who believed that a Socialist workers' revolution could be provoked to occur quickly in Russia.

While the Marxists were discussing future revolutions, workers in Russia were already fed up with their conditions. Throughout 1905, student demonstrations, workers' strikes, and peasant disorders erupted throughout the country in what became known as the Revolution of 1905. Tsar Nicholas II calmed the unrest by issuing a decree that allowed for some civil liberties and created a consultative legislative body, called a Duma. In October of that year, workers in St. Petersburg, the capital (known as Petrograd during the period 1914–1924), organized an elected council of workers, called a soviet, that served as a kind of municipal government. Similar soviets emerged in other cities.

The 1905 revolution was an important precursor to the Russian Revolution of 1917. It had exposed the people's dissatisfaction with the monarchy. The workers had come forward as a revolutionary class, able and willing to protest in support of their political and economic demands. And while the tsar severely limited the new legislature's authority, the Duma did present a counterbalance to the monarchy. In addition, the 1905 revolution produced the city soviets, which became a place for political discussions.

Workers' unrest continued sporadically throughout the next several years. Dissatisfaction also revolved around Russia's participation in World War I; in 1914 Russia had allied itself with France and England to fight Germany and Austria-Hungary. Russia's army was poorly prepared for war and had suffered terrible defeats. Shortages of food and fuel in the capital furthered public discontent.

In March 1917 (or February, by the Julian calendar that was used in Russia at the time, which is why it was called the February Revolution), the autocracy collapsed.

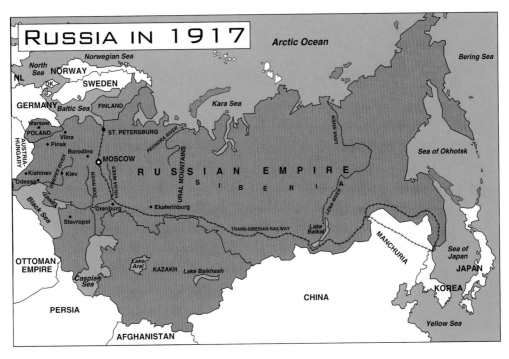

A demonstration in honor of International Women's Day erupted into a full-scale rally of peasants and workers angered by bread shortages and high prices. When the mob could not be controlled, members of the Duma and the tsar's staff suggested that Nicholas abdicate, or give up, the throne. Nicholas agreed and abdicated the throne to his brother, Grand Duke Michael, who declined the offer. The Duma decided that the government would be run by a self-appointed temporary body called the Provisional Government, until a Constituent Assembly could be elected by the people.

Because it failed to address the discontent among the peasants and workers swiftly and effectively, Russia's new government lasted only a few months. The Provisional Government found itself in a power struggle with the Petrograd Soviet of Workers' and Soldiers' Deputies, an elected body modeled after the 1905 soviet of workers. The soviet was in some cases more effective than the Provisional Government. It immediately set up a commission to cope with the problem of getting food supplies to the capital, placed revolutionary soldiers in government offices, and ordered the release of thousands of political prisoners.

The government did enact certain reforms such as disbanding the tsarist police forces and repealing limitations on freedom of opinion, press, association, and religion. With respect to crucial social problems, however, such as labor policy and

Soldiers and workers took control of the Russian government after the 1917 Russian revolution.

peasant land claims, the Provisional Government postponed major reforms for the decision of the future constituent assembly. The Petrograd soviet disagreed that labor and land issues could be postponed. In addition, the two bodies strongly disagreed about whether to continue Russia's participation in the war.

Members of the Red Guard, the military arm of the revolution, open fire from an armored car.

As the economy failed to improve, unrest in the lower classes continued. Vladimir Lenin and the Bolsheviks were ready to make the most of the workers' dissatisfaction and the inability of the government to rule effectively. On November 7 (or October 24, by the Julian calendar), the soviet's military revolutionary committee, the Red Guard, quickly occupied every key position in the capital, including government institutions, telegraph offices, railway stations, and bridges. They set up a roadblock in front of the Winter Palace, where the Provisional Government was in session.

Throughout the city, the Bolsheviks met almost no resistance; the streets were calm as people went about their normal daily activities.

A congress of soviets opened that evening and called for the transfer of power to the workers', soldiers', and peasants' soviets throughout the country. While the Bolsheviks did not enjoy an absolute majority, they were able to outwit other factions, and they announced that central governmental functions would be assumed by a new all-Bolshevik Council of People's Commissars. Lenin was later named its head.

Well after midnight, while the congress was in session, the Red Guard units made their final move on the Winter Palace. By this time, troops loyal to the government had dwindled, and the armed Bolsheviks made their way inside the building where they arrested the remaining ministers.

The October seizure of power was not the end of the story. While the Bolsheviks had easily taken control of Petrograd, they encountered resistance as they attempted to capture the rest of the country. In 1918, a bitter civil war erupted between the (Bolshevik) Reds and anti-Communist forces called the Whites. Over two years later, the Red Army was victorious. Lenin's Bolshevik faction renamed itself the Communist Party. The Communist Party ruled the country until the collapse of the Soviet Union in 1991.

GEORGE GAPON

LED WORKERS' MARCH THAT BEGAN 1905 REVOLUTION

George Gapon was born in the village of Beliki in Poltava, Ukraine, on February 5, 1870. He entered the priesthood in his early twenties and devoted himself to helping the poor.

In 1903, after moving to St. Petersburg, Gapon started an association of workers that met to address their harsh working conditions. At this time in Russia, factory workers toiled under difficult conditions; the average workday was over eleven hours long, and workers often endured unsafe and unhealthy conditions. In 1904, after prices rose for essential goods, Gapon led workers to strike. Over the next few days, over 110,000 workers refused to work. Gapon drafted a petition that outlined the workers' demands. They included an eight-hour workday, increased salaries, improved working conditions, freedom of speech, and an end to the Russo-Japanese War.

On January 22, 1905, Gapon led a peaceful parade of workers to the Winter Palace to present the petition and ask for Tsar Nicholas's assistance. Gapon and his followers fully believed that the tsar would come out to listen to their complaints. The workers carried religious icons and portraits of their beloved tsar as they marched toward his palace to beg for his help.

As it turned out, Nicholas II was not in the Winter Palace. Police opened fire on the crowd, killing about two hundred workers and wounding as many as eight hundred. Because of this bloodshed, the day became known as Bloody Sunday. Gapon's march on the Winter Palace and Bloody Sunday shattered the people's belief that the tsar was a kind dictator who always had their best interests in mind. The day sparked uprisings throughout the country for the next ten months. Workers refused to go to the factories, university students did not attend classes, and theater performances closed. Bloody Sunday and the turbulent year that followed it ruined the population's trust in the tsar.

After Bloody Sunday, Gapon first hid from tsarist police in St. Petersburg and then escaped across the border, ending up in Geneva, Switzerland. He joined the Socialist Revolutionary Party (SRP) but was suspected of spying on other Russian revolutionaries. Gapon was murdered by members of the SRP in March 1906 while visiting Finland.

Troops at the Winter Palace fired on George Gapon and striking factory workers on Bloody Sunday.

TSAR NICHOLAS II

RUSSIA'S FINAL TSAR

Nikolai Aleksandrovich Romanov was born on May 18, 1868, in Tsarskoye Selo, Russia. The eldest son of Russian tsar Alexander III and Empress Marie Romanova, Nicholas was crowned tsar of Russia upon the death of his father in 1894.

Nicholas married Princess Alix of Hesse-Darmstadt, to be known in Russia as Alexandra Romanova, just after his father's death. He came to depend heavily on her advice throughout his reign. Alexandra's continued reliance on an unkempt holy man named Rasputin caused concern among Russian citizens, who increasingly viewed Nicholas as a weak leader.

Tsar Nicholas II sits with his family for this photograph. Nicholas was forced from his throne in the 1917 revolution.

Nicholas's plans to expand the Russian empire into Manchuria and Korea spurred an unexpected attack from the Japanese navy in 1904, which set off war between the two countries. Russia suffered a terrible defeat in the Russo-Japanese War in 1905, which further damaged the prestige of the tsar.

At the same time that Russia was struggling in the Russo-Japanese War, Russian workers were struggling with poor conditions and long hours. After Bloody Sunday and the 1905 revolution, Nicholas calmed the country by issuing a decree called the October Manifesto. The October Manifesto provided for new liberties such as freedom of conscience, speech, meeting, and association, and the end of imprisonment without trial. In addition, Nicholas set up an elected and consultative body called the Duma that would be responsible for passing or rejecting Russia's laws. But the tsar retained full control of the country. In fact, Nicholas had the right to dissolve the Duma if he did not agree with its decisions, and he did so twice in its first two years.

At the outbreak of World War I in 1914, Russia found itself extremely unprepared for battle. As the war dragged on, Russia suffered defeat after crushing defeat. In September 1915, Nicholas felt it was his duty to lead his army directly, and he assumed the role of commander in chief. Russian troops continued to suffer losses that reflected poorly on their commander. Nicholas's popularity suffered further as Russian citizens called for an end to the war.

During the February Revolution of 1917, Nicholas ordered his troops to restore order. When the uprising could not be suppressed, Nicholas was forced to give up the throne. This marked the end of tsarist rule in Russia.

During his rule, Tsar Nicholas II repeatedly misjudged the depth of discontent in Russia. His many mistakes, such as leading ill-prepared troops into a disastrous world war, continuing to rule the Russian people with brute force and terror, and ignoring the Russian people's demands for reforms, ultimately brought about the collapse of the tsarist autocracy.

Nicholas and his family were sent to Ekaterinburg in Siberia, and they were killed by Bolsheviks on the night of July 16, 1918.

ALEXANDRA ROMANOVA

WIFE OF NICHOLAS II

T sarina Alexandra Feodorovna Romanova was born Alix Victoria Helena Louise Beatrice in Darmstadt, Germany, on June 6, 1872. She came from royal heritage; Louis IV, the Grand Duke of Hesse (Germany) was her father, and Queen Victoria of England was her grandmother.

Alexandra met the future tsar Nicholas II at the 1884 wedding of her sister Ella. The two married ten years later. Just after their wedding, Nicholas became Russia's tsar. Together Nicholas and Alexandra had five children—four daughters and one son, Alexei. Alexei, the heir to the monarchy, suffered from hemophilia, a serious blood disease that can cause uncontrollable bleeding.

Alexandra grew increasingly devoted to the Russian Orthodox Church and deeply superstitious. In 1905, she met Grigorii Rasputin, a peasant and holy man who claimed to have spiritual healing powers. Rasputin was successful in helping Alexei to stop bleeding, and he became an important member of the royal staff.

During World War I, when Nicholas traveled to the battlegrounds, Alexandra assumed control of state matters at home in Petrograd. Her faith in Rasputin led her to seek his advice not only in matters concerning her son but also on questions of state policy. Her dismissal of several liberal ministers in rapid succession

Nicholas II poses with Princess Alix of Hesse during their courtship (left). She and her five children (above) died at the hands of Bolsheviks in July 1918.

resulted in her increasing unpopularity; rumors even circulated that she and Rasputin were leaders of a pro-German group. Her bad decisions in state affairs and her reliance on the unpopular Rasputin contributed to the public dissatisfaction with the monarchy and quickened the end of tsarism in Russia.

After Nicholas II gave up the throne in 1917, the whole family was arrested and sent to the remote city of Ekaterinburg in Siberia. On July 16, 1918, Alexandra, Nicholas, and all five children were killed by Bolsheviks.

GRIGORII RASPUTIN

PEASANT HEALER WHO INFLUENCED ALEXANDRA

Rasputin, originally named Grigorii Yefimovich Novykh, was born into a peasant family in Siberia around 1869. At a young age he earned a reputation for wrongdoing and was called Rasputin, the Russian word for debauchery. Rasputin underwent a religious conversion at age eighteen. Later, he traveled to Greece and Jerusalem where he gained a reputation as a mystic and faith healer.

Rasputin moved to St. Petersburg and was referred to Tsar Nicholas and his wife Alexandra in order to aid their son Alexei, who suffered from a life-threatening blood disease. Because Rasputin was able to help the child, the tsar and tsarina welcomed him into the royal palace.

Rasputin's scandalous behavior throughout town fed rumors and brought shame to the royal family. Because the general public was not aware of Alexei's weak health and Rasputin's success in healing the boy, they could not understand why an illiterate and poorly behaved mystic would be accepted into the royal home.

As Nicholas became more and more involved in matters at the battlefield, Alexandra took a leading role in running state affairs at home. She turned to Rasputin for political advice. When Nicholas left for the front lines, Rasputin and the tsarina rapidly fired and appointed church and public officials, often replacing state ministers with incompetents and scoundrels who pledged their loyalty to Rasputin. Rumors spread that Rasputin and Alexandra were German spies, a serious criticism during wartime. Whether the rumors were true or not, it was clear to Nicholas's supporters that Rasputin was severely damaging the authority of the imperial government.

Appalled by Rasputin's influence over the tsarina and his disastrous effect on state policies, a group of aristocrats, led by Felix Yusupov, decided to murder him. Yusupov invited Rasputin to his home on December 29, 1916. After Rasputin arrived, Yusupov fed him poisoned cakes and wine. When Rasputin suffered no ill effects from the poison, Yusupov shot him. Later that evening, the group of nobles dropped Rasputin into the Neva River to make certain he was dead.

The murder of Rasputin was an attempt to save the credibility of the tsar, but the move came too late. If anything, the public had blamed Rasputin for many of the nation's ills, whereas after Rasputin's death, critics pointed directly at the tsar.

Rasputin's influence over the tsarina brought shame and scandal on the royal family.

RUSSIAN ARISTOCRAT WHO MURDERED RASPUTIN

Felix Yusupov was born on March 23, 1887, in St. Petersburg, to a very wealthy family. By age fifteen, Yusupov had been to many countries in Europe, and he studied in England at Oxford University.

In 1914, Yusupov married Irina, Tsar Nicholas's niece. Like many Russian nobles, Yusupov was convinced that Rasputin, the mystic adviser to the tsar's family, had too much control over the monarchy. In order to save the reputation of the tsar, Yusupov and three other men devised a plot to kill Rasputin.

Yusupov invited Rasputin to his estate for a party on December 29, 1916. Rasputin arrived, and although he consumed poisoned food and drink, they did not seem to have any harmful effect. Finally, frustrated and impatient, Yusupov took out a gun and shot Rasputin. Later Yusupov's coconspirators dropped Rasputin into the partially frozen Neva River to make certain he was dead.

Because of his close connection to the tsar, Yusupov was not punished for this crime. But his attempt to save the credibility of the tsar came too late. Rather than assisting the monarchy, Yusupov's removal of Rasputin served to quicken the end of tsarism. Without Rasputin to blame, the Russian public now criticized the tsar.

Russian aristocrat Felix Yusupov killed Rasputin to save the reputation of the tsar. At left, Yusupov poses with his wife Irina.

After the 1917 revolution, Yusupov sought exile in the United States. In 1953, he published his memoirs, which included details of Rasputin's murder and his role in it. Despite the fact that Rasputin had predicted that his murderer would live a short life, Yusupov lived to the age of eighty-one, dying in 1967.

ALEKSANDR KERENSKY

LEADER OF RUSSIA'S PROVISIONAL GOVERNMENT

Aleksandr Fedorovich Kerensky was born on April 22, 1881, in Simbirsk (now Ulyanovsk). In 1904, Kerensky graduated from St. Petersburg University, where he studied law. In 1905, he became the editor of a radical newspaper and was arrested. Released in 1906, he worked as a defense lawyer and developed a reputation for defending antitsarist revolutionaries.

In 1912, Kerensky was chosen as a deputy in the fourth state Duma. After the February Revolution, Kerensky and other members of the Duma created a provisional government. Initially, Kerensky assumed the position of minister of justice, but in July he was appointed prime minister. Kerensky's government introduced a number of progressive reforms, including abolishing the death penalty and introducing freedom of the press, speech, and religion. He also established an eight-hour workday for some jobs to relieve workers from exhausting conditions.

Although Kerensky successfully implemented some needed reforms, he failed to understand the depth of the discontent in the country, and his government lasted only a few months. The government did not address major complaints among peasants and workers, arguing that the Provisional Government was only a temporary body. The government made no concrete plans to redistribute land, which angered Russia's peasants. Kerensky also failed to address the economic situation; Russia's prices continued to rise. In addition, Kerensky pledged to continue the war effort, despite the public's disapproval. Kerensky's government continued to make mistakes, and the public's dissatisfaction with it allowed the Petrograd soviet and the Bolsheviks to gain strength and popularity.

Just before the planned elections for a new constituent assembly, Lenin and the Bolsheviks took over the government in the October Revolution. As troops surrounded the Winter Palace, Kerensky fled. Initially, he moved to Pskov, where he attempted to rally loyal troops to retake the capital. His troops captured Tsarskoye Selo, not far from Petrograd, but on the following day, they were defeated and Kerensky went into hiding.

Aleksandr Kerensky brought about many social reforms as head of the Provisional Government but failed to satisfy the public's unhappiness with the government's mistakes.

In June 1918, Kerensky managed to escape to France where he lived until 1940. After Germany defeated France in World War II, Kerensky traveled to the United States, eventually settling in New York City, where he died in 1970.

People scatter during intense street fighting between the Bolsheviks and troops loyal to Kerensky's Provisional Government.

GENERAL LAVR KORNILOV

COMMANDED PROVISIONAL GOVERNMENT'S ARMY

Lavr Georgievich Kornilov was born on August 30, 1870, in Ust-Kamenogorsk, Siberia. He studied at various military academies before being assigned to an artillery brigade in Turkestan in 1892. He had a prestigious and successful early career serving in India, Iran, Japan, and China.

After the 1917 February Revolution, Kornilov was assigned to restore order and discipline among the military forces in Petrograd. Displeased with his assignment, Kornilov resigned from this post and returned to the battlefield. Nevertheless, in early August, Kerensky, the prime minister of the Provisional Government, appointed Kornilov as commander in chief of the army.

In September, Kornilov sent troops into Petrograd to take control of the city. At first, Kerensky approved the maneuver, hoping that it would destroy the power of the Petrograd soviet and the Bolsheviks. However, at some point Kerensky came to believe that his commander in chief actually planned to use the troops to overthrow Kerensky's government and reinstate the tsar. Fearing for his own position, Kerensky called on the Bolsheviks for assistance. The Bolsheviks, unwilling to see a coup that would lead back to the tsarist system, decided to help in order to defend the revolutionary movement. The Petrograd soviet organized a military committee, and within a few days the Bolsheviks had enlisted twenty-five thousand armed men to defend Petrograd. Kornilov's troops backed down.

Lavr Kornilov, appointed commander in chief of the army by Kerensky, moved his troops into Petrograd but soon lost Kerensky's trust.

Historians disagree on whether Kornilov planned to use the troops to rescue the Provisional Government from the pressure of the soviet or whether he aimed to overthrow it. Whatever his motives, the Kornilov affair damaged Kerensky's reputation as a leader. Kerensky was blamed for allowing Kornilov to threaten counterrevolution and a possible return to tsarism. The soviet, on the other hand, emerged from the Kornilov affair with increased prestige; public support for the soviet had never been higher.

After the October Revolution, Kornilov became one of the commanders of the White Army during Russia's civil war. He was killed in military action in April 1918.

GEORGII VALENTINOVICH PLEKHANOV

FOUNDER OF RUSSIAN MARXISM

Georgii Valentinovich Plekhanov was born on December 11, 1856, in Gudalovka. As a young man, he joined a political group that demanded the relaxation of the strict tsarist regime. Because of his political beliefs, he was forced to leave Russia in 1880, and he spent most of his life in Geneva, Switzerland.

Georgii Valentinovich Plekhanov (third from right, opposite) founded Russian Marxism. Plekhanov believed revolution could not succeed without industrialization.

Known as the founder of Russian Marxism, Plekhanov began to study the theories of Karl Marx, translating some works into Russian. In doing so, he brought Marx's ideas of Socialist revolution to Russia, and these ideas provided the foundation for the October Revolution.

Vladimir Lenin became one of Plekhanov's followers. In 1900, Plekhanov and Lenin published the Socialist newspaper *Iskra* ("*Spark*"). This newspaper was printed in various European cities and smuggled into Russia by members of the Social Democratic Labor Party. In this newspaper and in published books, Plekhanov wrote that Russia would not be ready for socialism until the country had industrialized and experienced a period of capitalism.

After the Social Democratic Labor Party split into Menshevik and Bolshevik factions, Plekhanov worked to reunify the two factions. However, he kept control of *Iskra* and used it to criticize the tactics of Vladimir Lenin and the Bolsheviks. He even correctly predicted that if Lenin and the Bolsheviks ever gained full power in Russia, they would impose a dictatorship on the Russian people.

After the February Revolution of 1917, Plekhanov returned to Russia from exile in Switzerland, and he worked to gather support for continuing Russia's involvement in World War I, in opposition to the ideas and growing power of the Bolsheviks. After the Bolshevik overthrow of the government later that year, Plekhanov retired from public life. He died in 1918.

Karl Marx was born on May 5, 1818, in Trier, Germany. He studied law and philosophy at the University of Berlin and became interested in radicalism and political theory. After graduation, he worked as a journalist and editor. In 1843, Marx moved to Paris where he became involved with leaders of the revolutionary workers' movement. Marx came to believe that the sufferings of the working class could only be solved through socialism.

In Paris, Marx met Friedrich Engels, a German Socialist philosopher, and the two became lifelong collaborators. Together they researched, edited, and wrote materials about socialism that urged the working class to rise up in revolution.

In 1848, they published the *Communist Manifesto*, which demanded a Communist society that would include an end to private property, the nationalization of farmland and factories, and free public schools, among other things. These notions would become crucial components of the Soviet system after 1922.

Within weeks of the *Manifesto*'s publication, revolutions broke out in France, Italy, and Austria. Marx returned to Germany but was later deported for publishing a revolutionary newspaper. He went to London in August 1849. His

Karl Marx (right) and Friedrich Engels (left) wrote and published the Communist Manifesto. *Marx's Socialist philosophy influenced the revolution's leaders.*

publication of *Das Kapital*, a three-volume study of capitalism, was translated into Russian in 1872 and published despite tsarist censors. The book was extremely popular in Russia, especially among intellectuals. Although Marx had argued that Russia was not ready for revolution because of its unindustrialized state, he admitted that his work was most valued and read in Russia. Despite the income from his Russian book sales, Marx lived in poverty and experienced declining health. He died in 1883.

Marx was important to Vladimir Lenin. Lenin adapted the German's ideas to the Russian context, arguing that a Socialist revolution of workers and peasants could be brought about without the industrialization of Russia. He successfully implemented this idea in the October Revolution.

VLADIMIR LENIN

LEADER OF THE OCTOBER REVOLUTION

Vladimir Lenin was born Vladimir Ilyich Ulyanov in Simbirsk (now Ulyanovsk), on April 22, 1870. In May 1887, his oldest brother was hanged for participating in a plot to kill Tsar Alexander III, an event that inspired the young Lenin to become a revolutionary.

Lenin moved to St. Petersburg in 1893 and became deeply interested in Marxism. Arrested for his involvement in organizing a workers' trade union, Lenin was held in prison for a year, then sent to Siberia where he remained in exile until 1900.

After returning from exile, Lenin spent a great deal of time in Europe to avoid tsarist arrest. Together with Georgii Plekhanov, Lenin started a revolutionary newspaper called *Iskra* ("*Spark*"), and wrote books and materials to spread the socialist message. Throughout the next several years, he continued to travel, to participate in socialist meetings, and to write revolutionary materials.

After the February Revolution, Lenin prepared to return to Russia. When he arrived in Petrograd (formerly St. Petersburg) in April, he was greeted by tens of thousands of workers and soldiers. Speaking to the excited mobs, he argued that the Provisional Government did not represent the welfare of the Russian masses who needed a radically new Socialist society.

Spurred on by Lenin's return, the Bolsheviks were no longer interested in cooperating with the Provisional Government. A large workers' uprising in July, however, found the Bolsheviks yet unready to challenge the government for power. After the uprising was contained, the government renewed its repression of Bolshevik members, and Lenin fled to Finland.

By early September, however, the Bolsheviks had won victories in the Moscow and Petrograd soviets, and party membership rose from 60,000 in July to 250,000. Despite being in Finland, Lenin was able to exert considerable influence through letters that called for a Bolshevik-led armed uprising against the Provisional Government.

When he returned later in September, Lenin persuaded the leaders of the Bolshevik Party to adopt his idea for revolution. The party began to train Red Guard units and to visit factories and garrisons to promote the revolution.

Vladimir Lenin led the Bolsheviks and was the driving force behind the October Revolution of 1917.

With a congress of soviets scheduled to meet in Petrograd on November 7, 1917, Lenin insisted that the takeover must take place on the same day. On the morning of November 7, all Bolshevik newspapers ran headlines that declared all power to the soviets. Later that day, Bolshevik forces took over the Winter Palace.

Although he was behind the scenes during the takeover, Lenin had clearly provided the inspiration for the maneuver. Lenin's unfaltering belief in the revolutionary cause, his inspiring speeches and writings, and his reliance on party discipline persuaded others to follow him to revolution.

Lenin was elected the head of the new government. After a bloody civil war, Lenin created the Union of Soviet Socialist Republics, or the USSR. Lenin suffered the first of four strokes in 1922 and died in 1924 at the age of fifty-four.

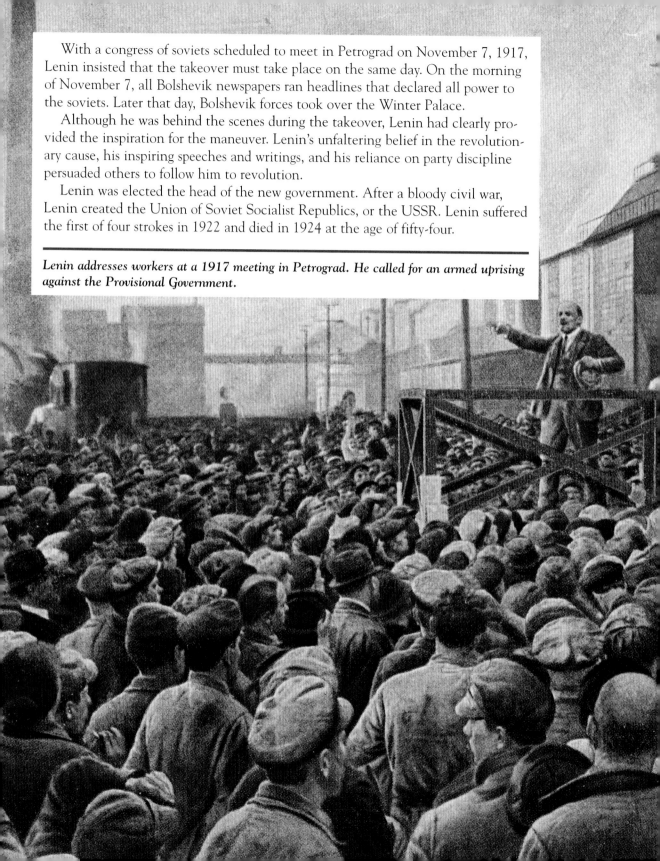

Lenin addresses workers at a 1917 meeting in Petrograd. He called for an armed uprising against the Provisional Government.

LEON TROTSKY

TRAINED TROOPS WHO OVERTHREW THE PROVISIONAL GOVERNMENT

Leon Trotsky was born Lev Davidovich Bronstein in Yanovka, Ukraine, on November 7, 1879. He became interested in Marxism at a young age, and by 1896 he had joined the Social Democrats. Trotsky was arrested in 1898 because of his work organizing a workers' union. He was imprisoned for two years and was then sentenced to four years in exile in Siberia. He escaped from Siberian exile in 1902 and traveled to England.

In England, Trotsky met Vladimir Lenin and Georgii Plekhanov, and he began to write articles for the newspaper *Iskra* (Spark). In 1903, he attended the Second Congress of the Social Democratic Labor Party, and when the party split, he strongly opposed Lenin and sided with the Mensheviks.

By 1905, Trotsky had returned to Russia and was elected chairman of the St. Petersburg soviet. Because he was active in the 1905 revolution, he was exiled again to Siberia, this time for life, but he again managed to escape. While in exile, Trotsky lived in various cities in Europe and kept deeply involved in the revolutionary movement. He wrote about a permanent Socialist revolution, explaining that a revolution in Russia would be followed by similar revolutions in other countries throughout the world. This would become an important goal of the Communist Party in later years.

During World War I, Trotsky led the Mensheviks in denouncing Russia's involvement in the war. When the 1917 February Revolution broke out in Petrograd, he returned to Russia and, despite his opposition to Lenin in earlier years, joined the Bolshevik Party and was appointed to its Central Committee. When Lenin went into hiding in July, Trotsky rose to lead the revolutionary movement, mobilizing support using his talents as a gifted speaker and organizer. In October, he became the leader of the Petrograd soviet, and he also served as the chair of the Revolutionary Military Committee. In this capacity, Trotsky recruited and trained troops, known as the Red Guard, to overthrow the Provisional Government.

As head of the Revolutionary Military Committee, Leon Trotsky organized the Red Guard to force out the Provisional Government.

Soon after the Bolsheviks took power, Trotsky was named commissar of war. As such, he singlehandedly built up and molded the Red Guard into a 5-million-member Red Army that was victorious over the Whites in Russia's civil war. When Lenin died, Trotsky hoped to become the Soviet Union's next leader, but he lost out to Stalin.

Trotsky and his supporters fought within the Communist Party against Stalin's leadership for several years. Stalin could not tolerate the competition. In 1927 Trotsky was ejected from the Communist Party; in 1928 he was sent into exile; and in 1929 he and his family were deported from the Soviet Union. Trotsky and his family eventually settled in Mexico, where he was brutally murdered in his home by Stalin's assassins on August 20, 1940.

Trotsky's disagreements with Stalin's policies led to Trotsky's exile to Mexico, where Stalin's assassin's murdered him in 1940.

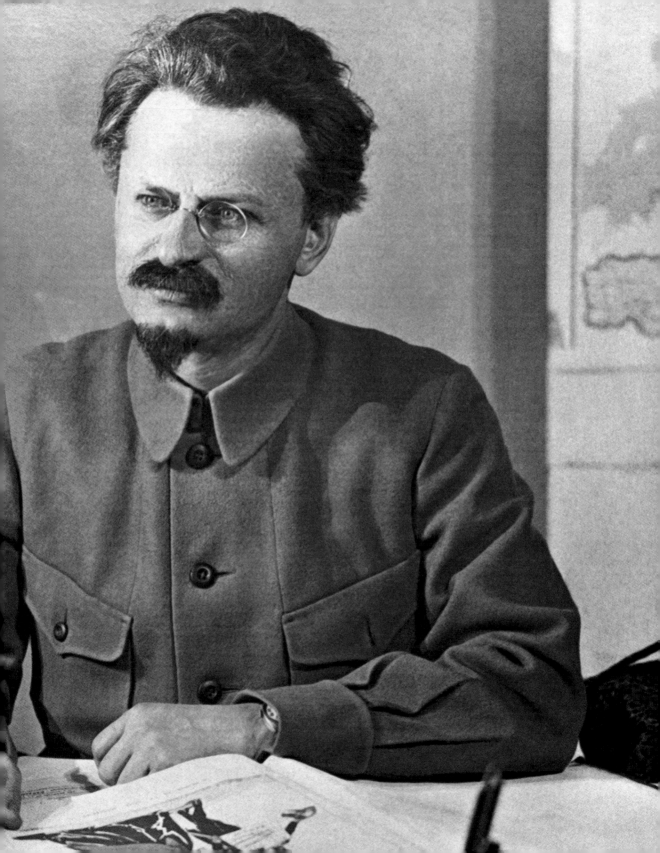

VLADIMIR MAYAKOVSKY

RUSSIAN REVOLUTIONARY POET

Vladimir Mayakovsky was born in Bagdadi (later named Mayakovsky), Georgia, on July 19, 1893. In 1906, his family moved to Moscow, and two years later Mayakovsky joined the Bolshevik faction of the Social Democratic Labor Party. That year, he was arrested for rebellious activities and put in prison for eleven months. During his jail term, Mayakovsky read continually and began to write poetry.

After his release, the young poet joined the Russian Futuristic movement. The movement was composed of writers, painters, musicians, and theater directors who sought to break from cultural traditions. Mayakovsky moved to St. Petersburg in 1912 where he and others Futurists roamed the streets in costumes, or with painted faces, and broke up traditional social and art gatherings by shouting or throwing things. The Futurists' timing was ideal; discontent with the tsarist society allowed the movement to gain popularity, setting an example for other artists to try new things.

Mayakovsky's modern poetry and disregard for cultural traditions provide an example of how Bolshevik thinking permeated nearly every aspect of Russian society. Mayakovsky supported the Bolshevik ideals and even volunteered his artistic skills to assist the Bolsheviks during the civil war by writing poems such as "Ode to Revolution" and "Left March." Known as the poet of the revolution, from 1919 to 1921 he designed hundreds of propaganda posters that called for Bolshevik victory. He also wrote short plays and commercial jingles for state enterprises. Mayakovsky's endorsement of the Bolsheviks separated him from many of his colleagues, who either left Russia or were silenced by Communist censors.

In time, Mayakovsky became increasingly disillusioned about the Soviet system under the brutal dictatorship of Joseph Stalin. He wrote two plays, *The Bedbug* (1928) and *The Bathhouse* (1930), both of which presented absurd and funny plots on the surface but actually harshly criticized the Soviet system.

Mayakovsky committed suicide in Moscow on April 14, 1930. After his death, a wave of grief swept the country. Stalin attempted to make the most of the poet's popularity by calling him the best poet of the Soviet epoch. The dictator even declared indifference to Mayakovsky's writings to be a state crime.

Vladimir Mayakovsky supported Bolshevik ideals in his poetry and became known as the poet of the revolution. He later became critical of Soviet politics.

JOHN REED

AMERICAN JOURNALIST AND COMMUNIST

John Reed was an American radical writer and poet. He was born in Portland, Oregon, on October 20, 1887. The son of an insurance salesman, he received his bachelor's degree from Harvard University in 1910. Reed later joined a group of radical writers living in New York City's Greenwich Village and began working as a journalist.

Journalist John Reed (fourth from left) attends a political meeting in Russia. He wrote a firsthand account of the revolution and later helped found the American Communist Labor Party.

In early 1917 he married Louise Bryant, and together they traveled to Russia to witness and report on the October Revolution in Petrograd. Both Reed and Bryant were captivated by the Bolsheviks. The couple socialized with Lenin and other Bolshevik leaders and greatly respected them.

In 1919, Reed published a book entitled *Ten Days That Shook the World*. The book focused on the October Revolution and the crucial days when Lenin incited the Bolsheviks to seize power from the Provisional Government. It provides a unique first-hand account that includes political conversations and arguments among the leading figures.

After returning to the United States, Reed helped to found the American Communist Labor Party and worked as the first editor of the leftist journal *Voice of Labor*. After charges of treason in the United States, he fled to Finland. Finnish authorities held him before releasing him to Russia in exchange for Russian-held Finnish prisoners of war.

In Russia, Reed was able to contact Bryant, who joined him. In 1920, Reed contracted typhus and died on October 19. He was buried with other Bolshevik heroes beside the wall of the Kremlin, the building complex that housed the Soviet government. Reed's life as a radical leader was the subject of the 1981 film *Reds*.

JOSEPH STALIN

LENIN'S SUCCESSOR WHO BECAME A RUTHLESS DICTATOR

Joseph Stalin was born Joseph Vissarinovich Dzhugashvili on December 21, 1879, in the Caucasian region of the Russian empire, now Georgia. Stalin first became interested in socialism in 1899, and from 1902 to 1917 he was repeatedly arrested because of his underground work with the Bolsheviks.

Stalin met Lenin for the first time in 1905 in Finland. Although Leon Trotsky and other Bolsheviks did not care for Stalin, Lenin was impressed with Stalin's total commitment to the party. Stalin was so devoted to the Bolshevik cause that he even robbed banks to enhance the party's income. Because of this loyalty, Stalin was appointed to the Bolshevik Central Committee in January 1912.

As a result of his own humble background, Stalin understood the peasants in a way that Lenin and the other intellectuals could not. His insight into the peasants' views on land ownership assisted Lenin in crafting a platform that attracted the support of the peasant class.

During the February Revolution, Stalin was returning to Petrograd from exile in Siberia. He played only a minor role in the Bolshevik seizure of power, but he proved himself a loyal Bolshevik and a faithful supporter of Lenin. After the October Revolution, he was appointed political commissar of the Soviet army during Russia's civil war.

In 1922, he was elected by the Communist Party as its general secretary, a position that he later developed into the most powerful position in the Soviet Union. Lenin foresaw this and, before his death, called for Stalin's removal because he felt that Stalin had already gained too much power.

After Lenin's death in 1924, a power struggle ensued among Stalin, Leon Trotsky, and others over who would become the next leader. Eventually Stalin outmaneuvered his rivals. Lenin and the Bolsheviks had shown their ability to use brutal force, and Stalin adapted their techniques as he went on to become one of the world's most cruel and terrifying dictators. In the ten years after 1929, Stalin quickly industrialized the Soviet Union at the expense of millions of lives. His forced collectivization of agriculture, in which farmland and assets were

Joseph Stalin's humble background gave him insight to peasant views. He became the Communist Party's most powerful leader.

transferred into collective or state ownership rather than private ownership, resulted in famine in the 1930s, and more than 10 million people died. During the "Great Purge," he imprisoned, sent to labor camps, and executed millions of Soviet citizens, for little or no reason. Stalin's executions were carried out against everyday citizens as well as countless Bolsheviks and governmental officials.

Stalin's industrialization efforts allowed the country to construct a mighty military that defeated Nazi German troops during World War II. The Soviet Union emerged as a world superpower that battled the United States for global influence throughout the next forty-five years. Stalin ruled the Soviet Union until his death at age seventy-three on March 5, 1953.

Stalin (left) adopted the brutal methods of the Bolsheviks under Lenin (below left), shown here with fellow revolutionary Mikhail Kalinin. Stalin had more than 10 million Soviet citizens executed.

May 1894	Tsar Nicholas II begins his reign in Russia after the death of his father, Alexander III.
July 1903	Russian Social Democratic Labor Party splits into Bolshevik and Menshevik factions.
1904–1905	Russia and Japan engage in the Russo-Japanese War.
January 1905	Tsarist troops open fire on peaceful demonstration of workers led by George Gapon in St. Petersburg, resulting in over 130 deaths. This day becomes known as Bloody Sunday.
January–October 1905	Bloody Sunday sparks student demonstrations, workers' strikes, and peasant uprisings throughout Russia.
October 1905	Tsar Nicholas II issues the October Manifesto, which gives some civil liberties and sets up a Duma, a consultative legislative body. Workers in St. Petersburg organize an elected council of workers, called a soviet.
August 1914	Russia joins France and England to fight against Germany and Austria-Hungary in World War I.
December 1916	Grigorii Rasputin is killed.
February–March 1917	A demonstration in honor of International Women's Day erupts into full-scale unrest. Tsar Nicholas II abdicates the throne. The Duma sets up a Provisional Government to lead Russia until an elected Constituent Assembly can be created.
July 1917	Aleksandr Kerensky becomes new prime minister of the Provisional Government. Leon Trotsky joins the Bolshevik Party.
September 1917	General Kornilov sends troops into Petrograd seemingly to confront the power of the Petrograd soviet. When Kerensky comes to believe that this is actually an attempted overthrow of the Provisional Government, he calls on the soviet for help.

Leaders of the new, postrevolution Russian parliament pose for a 1917 photograph. Their leader, Aleksandr Kerensky, stands second from right.

September–October 1917	The Bolsheviks win control of the Petrograd soviet. Trotsky becomes head of the Petrograd soviet.
November 1917	The Bolsheviks overthrow the Provisional Government on the eve of the meeting of a congress of soviets. Kerensky flees Petrograd. Lenin heads the new Council of People's Commissars.
Summer 1918	Russian civil war begins.
July 1918	Nicholas II and family are killed by Bolsheviks in Ekaterinburg.
November 1920	White Army is defeated and the civil war ends.
January 1924	Vladimir Lenin dies.

FOR FURTHER INFORMATION

BOOKS

Robert Goldston, *The Fall of the Winter Palace: November 1917, Old Russia's Tsardom Is Swept Away by Bolshevik Revolution*. New York: Franklin Watts, 1971.

————, *The Russian Revolution*. London: Phoenix House, 1966.

Ted Gottfried, *The Road to Communism: The Rise and Fall of the Soviet Union*. Brookfield, CT: Twenty-First Century, 2002.

John J. Vail, *"Peace, Land, Bread!": A History of the Russian Revolution*. New York: Facts On File, 1996.

Susan Willoughby, *The Russian Revolution*. Crystal Lake, IL: Rigby Interactive Library, 1996.

WEB SITES

Russian History Website (www.alexanderpalace.org).
This Web site includes a lot of information in text form. It focuses exclusively on Russian history and culture under the tsars.

Geographica (www.geographia.com).
The section on Russia includes a brief narrative history on Russia's path to revolution and the Soviet period.

Marxist Internet Archive (www.marxists.org).
This Internet archive gives information on Marxism and Marxist writers and includes discussion of the Russian Revolution and Soviet period.

Spartacus Educational Website (www.spartacus.schoolnet.co.uk).
This Web site includes a lot of information on the actions and issues surrounding the Russian Revolution as well as other historical events. There are also biographies of a large number of Russian revolutionaries and foreign witnesses, and explanations of various political groups of the period.

ABOUT THE AUTHOR

Britta Bjornlund is a program manager at the Library of Congress where she runs a large exchange program for leaders from Russia and other parts of the former Soviet Union. She has authored three books on the Cold War. Ms. Bjornlund holds a master's degree in international relations from the Johns Hopkins University School of Advanced International Studies (SAIS) and a bachelor's degree from Williams College, where she majored in Russian. She lives in Washington, D.C.

INDEX